Master of Gay-Dar - My High School Romance Caught Up With Me In College

How I struggled, and Confused About my sexuality, how you too can know, and how to safely 'come out'

Saxon Clive

TABLE OF CONTENTS

CHAPTER ONE

MY ENCOUNTER WITH BRIAN

It was summer in college, and like every other freshman, I tried to blend in, avoiding the existing students, in order to either stay out of trouble or avoid insults and embarrassments that is uncalled for. I know you know what I'm saying. Every school in the United States have in one way or the other, those group that would bully that 'seemingly intelligent' student. I have come to realize that they mostly do this because they either lack love, want to feel in charge and powerful, or just a random douchebag. You may have your different theory, but these are my analyses, and personal experience and conclusion.

I was assigned a room where I have to stay with this lovely freshman. He has a curly dark hair, deep blue eyes, tall, soft-looking skin (I haven't touched and felt it at the moment), his shoulders are just the right size, he had sexy buttocks cos he was bending over, and unpacking his bag. His legs are to compete for, straight and athletic.

'Hi, I'm Clive" I stuttered while stretching my hands for a shake

"Hey mann, I'm Brian" He turned and responded enthusiastically "Bring it in, Bud, I'm a huger" He softly put my hand down and gave me a hug

His perfume shut my eyes and brain for a second. He smelled so good, I held him like it was my last hug on earth.

"Mmuahh" He kissed me on the cheek

"Ohhm keeps getting better" I muttered under my breath.

I have found other boys attractive in the past, but I wasn't sure what I felt.

You know that feeling when you're in-between the drunk, and sober thin-line?

You'll question yourself if you are behaving right, and you strongly affirm that you are sober, and know exactly what you are doing, and sometimes, you are just totally messed up without even knowing it.

That was my situation.

I knew I was liking these random boys, but it hardly got emotional, I probably just love how he pronounces "Lingerie" or I just love that he's smart. There's always a reason for my connection.

For Brian, it was something instantaneous, and stronger than anything I have ever felt before.

Ok, take a chill pill, let me take you on a journey back in time, before the whole college saga, that is already blowing up before it started.

In school, it took a significant amount of time and energy to get me to blend in. I hardly talked to my classmates.

Before then, my parents noticed how this is affecting others around me. They would take me to dinner gathering with others, I could barely say a word, and when I'm asked a question, I respond with just one word.

I wanted to change that, I really wanted to but it wasn't just my person. I have been taken to Psychologists, all I did was piss them off with my awful silence, and I will end up getting transferred to another.

I wasn't interested in what the boys were interested in. I couldn't give two fucks about football, hanging out and getting high or even frats.

I was quiet lion. I remember when Cayle thought he could bully me because of my quietness, I gave him the taste of his own medicine that he had to transfer to another school.

Before graduation and prom, I was really confused about my sexuality. I had some weird inexplicable feelings, and urges. I know I don't have relaxed deep voice like the gents that I know, but it could've happened to anyone, right?

Not all gay people have high-pitched voice though.

In class, I have always had a thing for Josh. Josh is so smart and he always say he'll take over the world's finance one day. I don't even know what that means, and I care-less. There's this thing he does with his hair, and every time he does this, it just seems like time slowed, every damn time.

Well, he didn't know I liked him like that. Yes, I'm a classic stalker.

I look at him in the class, hallway, school bus, changing room, library and every other corner.

Well, about what I said earlier about him not knowing, not until prom night. I hate gatherings, but I particularly excitedly attended in time because I know I would be seeing Josh, and hopefully, not for the last.

Long story short, he asked for a dance, out of nowhere, I even had to look back and point to myself, just to make sure he was referring to me. He nodded in affirmation. I almost shouted, and announced it to everybody who care to listen.

Instead, I calmly walked towards him, acting like I wasn't interested when it was the best day of my life.

I started dancing really violently - excitement was filled in the air. When I felt a hand around my waist. I melted. I couldn't explain what these feelings are, and why I'm feeling them towards same gender.

Josh's hand around my waist did something to me. I could feel my spine take a different shape, my shoulders shuddered, I could hear the loud noise my throat made, my eyes suddenly wanted to forcefully close.

I managed to stay strong on the dancing floor, I held his shoulder.

"Damnn, Lordd" This was all I could mutter under my breath.

I could smell the baby powder fragrance on Josh, and I suddenly forgot my name. I got mesmerized that I didn't know when the music ended, I was still having my arms crossed around his supple neck, and head rested on his right shoulder.

He shook me awake from my fantasy world

"Hey, the music is ended, we're ready for the main event" He calmly whispered

I didn't move cos it felt like I heard it in my dreams. But his voice came at me again, this time, a little closer

"You know, if you wanna dance more after the event, there would be music for us" He said chuckling.

"Huh" I said raising my head

"Ohh, I'm so sorry, of course" I said, behaving like I'm dusting off thing from my clothes, still embarrassed.

"Don't be sorry, I was enjoying the dance, but clearly not as you were" He said, smiling.

Ohh, those smiles. There's thing thing that happens with his eye brows when he smiles, it's just everything you would want to dream about for a restful night.

That was the last time I saw Josh.

What happened? Life did.

It's the same thing about to happen with Brian?

I hope not.

The first day was awesome, but the ensuing days took strength, discipline and self talk to get through. It was becoming clearer with every action that I'm actually gay.

For a long time, I was in denial, and deep in the closet because I wouldn't want things that happen to people who are, happen to me, especially in high school.

Brian was a 'free man,' he would sleep and stay in the room naked, dangling his instrument of destruction from left to the right.

He was really a fine man, and in some moments, with a book in front of me, all I could think of is going down on Brian, and licking the life out of him.

I'm very attractive to ladies, but I almost never seem to notice their advances. Beatrice, of my French class mates had to tell me that I was the dumbest human alive in reading ladies' green light.

"When I have a red light in my room?" I thought in my head, while offering an apology.

"I don't want any distractions, I just wanna focus on my studies" I politely said to her "And Brian" I added in my head, and smiled.

I started noticing Brian checking me out, and looking with desires in his eyes. He never came off like someone who was into same gender, and I honestly didn't know how to tell.

I started responding with same look and gaze, and we were like a month into college, and living together.

This one time after class, I chose to remain bare and trust that his butt will return. I was situated, backing the entryway, and was seeing some paper works. When he came in and shut the entryway, I felt his hand on my shoulders, it was firm, delicate, and stress-alleviating! I turned right away, looked at him without flinching and I let him kiss me and he went down on me… I began groaning boisterously, which made him laugh. He requested that I hold the commotion down so as not to alarm anybody outside… the entire thing turned me on!

Whenever we finished, I understood this is only the start of something truly unique.

Half a month after the fact he welcomed me to return home with him, which transformed into a long supernatural sex-filled excursion, which turned into my first time; I was so captivated by him that I gave him my prudence and cherished each and every moment of it.

CHAPTER TWO

HOW CAN I DISCERN IF I'M GAY

Before you start your Freudian psychoanalysis, confirm to say that you simply have a 'gay-dar', and don't forget to detail how accurate it is and has always been. Frame it as an insurmountable achievement of yours. After all, it's far more prestigious than being awarded a Harvard Fellow. There's no reason to believe the reliability or accuracy of your data collection because you don't have any, so just launch straight in.

Not everybody are often a gay or lesbian. there's a selected skill to identifying those folks who are. Here are some tell-tale signs that somebody may be a gay or lesbian:

The first thing to require note of when deciding someone's sexuality on their behalf, namely whether a person is gay or not, is to watch how high-pitched their voice is. The more high-pitched their usual speaking voice is, the more likely it's that you simply are lecture a gay person. this is often because the pitch of your voice has nothing to try to to with biology: it's actually determined by your sexuality. Forget what scientists say – they're all just conspiracy theorists, really.

The second hint to require note of is that if they use excessive hand gestures, then they probably are gay. The key to the present one is that if you're a person who is interested in another man, you'll tend to maneuver your hands around quite often more than a typical person when speaking. this is often evidenced by how the branches of trees tend to wave around more outside within the wind than indoors. It's an equivalent logic as why witches, like Connie Booth, will weigh the maximum amount as a duck does. These species of citizenry also tend to be well-groomed, wear strong cologne and luxuriate in getting to gay bars. Just check out Christian Stovitz. Just imagine the gay man in Clueless, how wrong can you be? the answer is: not likely. Hollywood is essentially the great encyclopedia to understanding the range of minority communities within our society.

As for spotting lesbians, they're going to be more likely than not to have short hair, refuse to shave and wear bras, also as be a neighborhood of the feminism . They also enjoy declaring their distaste for penises every five minutes of any conversation about politics, the economy or physics . They graze in small herds and have a tendency to be too busy reading The Vagina Monologues and braiding their underarm hair to worry that you simply don't think the patriarchy exists. Lesbians also commonly have tattoos and piercings on every ten square centimetres of skin area. She's got a tongue piercing? Definitely a lesbian. this is often a flawless application of modus ponens logic; you ought to be proud.

Now, continuing together with your analysis: if they're not white, then they're probably not gay or lesbian. Just take a glance at Legally Blonde, Modern Family, Glee, Orange is that the New Black, Girls, Easy A, and therefore the list of films and television shows with homosexual side characters. All the gay and lesbian characters are white. So, if you're someone of colour, how are you able to possibly be gay or lesbian? Don't be too trapped in diversity; remember that each characteristic of an individual is a clear hint to the mystery of compressing them into a category of gender, ethnicity or sexuality.

Unlike their heterosexual peers who come from diverse backgrounds and have a plethora of private interests intricately woven into the material of their lives, the lifetime of a homosexual will revolve around their sexuality. consistent with Hollywood, it'll run something like this – you'll spend the primary several years of your life struggling to understand that you're not straight, then subsequent few years beginning and expecting people to simply accept your 'new' identity (that was never really new). Then, you'll spend the remainder of your life doing something that revolves around being a homosexual.

You know you'll make certain that someone's a homosexual once they fit all of those descriptions. It's not like all three-dimensional person could fit into your one-dimensional description of a gay or lesbian. After all, they're a minority, so it's pretty uncommon to ascertain one around. the sole reasonable thing to try is to assume most are straight until they perfectly fit this description. Don't acknowledge that folks can produce other qualities and interests outside of your understanding of them. It's an excessive amount of for the brain to handle on top of getting to work out what you're getting to do with the remainder of your life after university.

When you are concluding your end , make certain to present yourself as a hero. Without your wisdom, how would the remainder folks be ready to identify those folks who are gay and lesbian from those that aren't , end world poverty, eradicate all human rights abuses and stop our globally warming planet from descending into chaos?

CHAPTER THREE

ACCEPTANCE

It's normal to feel interested in both girls and boys when you're growing up. determine about beginning , safer sex, and the way to affect bullying if it happens to you.

During puberty, you've got many emotions and sexual feelings. It's normal for women to believe girls during a sexual way, and for boys to believe boys during a sexual way.

Some people realize they like people of the other sex, while others feel they like people of an equivalent sex. Some people realize they're gay, lesbian or bisexual at an early age, while others might not know until later in life.

Some children can also be confused about their sexual identity. they'll be asexual, where you are not curious about sex in the least , or transgender, where people believe there's a mismatch between their biological sex and identity as a boy or girl.

You do not choose your sexuality, it chooses you. Nobody knows what makes people gay, lesbian, bisexual or trans. Whatever your sexuality, you need to be with someone you're keen on .

What if I'm gay, lesbian or bisexual?

It can help to speak to people who are going through an equivalent thing., determine if there is a young men's or women's group in your area for lesbian, gay or bisexual people.

These groups could be advertised at GP surgeries, sexual health or contraceptive clinics, pharmacies, youth groups, local papers, or on the web .

Find sexual health services, including contraceptive clinics, near you.

Should I tell anyone I feel I'm gay, lesbian or bisexual?

This is up to you. Being gay, lesbian or bisexual is normal, but some people don't understand this. Telling people you're gay, lesbian or bisexual is understood as beginning .

When you first begin , the foremost sensible option is to inform someone you trust, and who are going to be supportive and understanding.

If you are not sure how you are feeling about your sexuality, there is no hurry to form your mind up or tell people.

Coming out is a private decision, and it is vital to try to to it in your own way and in your own time.

What about sex if I'm gay, lesbian or bisexual?

We all have an equivalent feelings and anxieties about sex. Deciding when you're able to roll in the hay may be a big step, whatever your sexuality and whoever your potential partner could be .

Everyone is ready at different times, but don't roll in the hay simply because your mates or your boyfriend or girlfriend are pressuring you. Remember, it is often okay to say no.

You can also read Are you ready for sex? to seek out out the items to ask yourself if you're brooding about having sex.

If you think that the time is true , ask your partner about wanting to use contraception, having safer sex, picking the proper time, and the way you'd both just like the experience to be.

STIs with someone of an equivalent sex

If you're having sex with someone of an equivalent sex, there is no risk of pregnancy, but sexually transmitted infections (STIs) can pass from girls to women and boys to boys, also as between girls and boys.

If you're using sex toys, cover them with a condom and use a replacement condom whenever – condoms should only be used once. Boys should wear a condom if they need oral or sodomy .

Make sure you recognize about all the methods of contraception, whether you've got sex with males or females, just in case you furthermore may have straight sex. It's better to be prepared with contraception than to place yourself in danger . Always use condoms to stop STIs.

HOW TO FACE GAY BULLIES

How to cope if you're bullied for being gay.

Some people don't understand that being gay, lesbian or bisexual is normal. Nobody has the proper to inform somebody else the way to live their life or pick on them due to who they're interested in .

If someone bullies you because you're gay, lesbian or bisexual, it's their problem, not yours, and that they shouldn't escape with it. this is often called homophobic bullying.

Bullying can take many forms, including stares, looks, whispers, threats and violence. If you're being bullied because you're gay, lesbian or bisexual, tell someone you trust. this might be an educator , friend, your parents, or a helpline.

Schools have a duty to make sure homophobic bullying is addressed . determine more from the Anti-Bullying Alliance on where to seek out help if you have been bullied for advice.

You'll find information about lecture teachers and parents, and therefore the contact details of anti-bullying organization and helplines. lecture someone who is knowing will always help if you've got worries or questions as you'll feel supported and more confident.

Sorting out your direction can be confounded.

In a general public where the vast majority of us are supposed to be straight, it very well may be challenging to make a stride back and find out if you're gay, straight, or something different.

You're the main individual who can sort out what your direction genuinely is.

Everything began with a sex dream - is this serious about what I think it implies?

A considerable lot of us grow up to expect that we're straight just to find out, later, that we're not.

Now and again, we understand this since we have intercourse dreams, sexual thoughts, or sensations of serious fascination toward individuals of similar orientation as us.

Notwithstanding, none of those things - sex dreams, sexual considerations, or even sensations of extreme fascination - essentially "demonstrate" your direction.

Having a sex drive for an individual of a similar orientation as you doesn't guarantee to make you gay. Having a sex drive for a person of the opposite orientation doesn't be guaranteed to make you straight.

There are one or two types of fascination. With regards to orientation, we for the most part allude to heartfelt fascination (who you have solid heartfelt affections for and want a close connection with) and physical allure (who you need to participate in sexual escapades with).

Once in a while we're sincerely and physically drawn to similar gatherings. Some of the time we're not.

For instance, it's feasible to be sincerely drawn to men however physically drawn to men, ladies, and non-binary individuals. This kind of circumstance is designated "blended direction" or "cross direction" - and it's absolutely alright.

Each and every straight individual is special. Each and every gay individual is special. Each individual, of each direction, is special.

You don't need to satisfy certain "measures" to qualify as gay, straight, sexually unbiased, or whatever else.

This is a part of your personality, not a request for employment - and you can relate to anything that term fits you!

Then how could I know?

There's no "correct" method for dealing with your direction. Be that as it may, there are a couple of things you can do to investigate your sentiments and assist with sorting out things.

Regardless of anything else, let yourself feel your sentiments. It's difficult to get your sentiments in the event that you overlook them.

Indeed, even presently, there's a ton of disgrace and shame around direction. Individuals who aren't straight are regularly caused to feel like they ought to quell their sentiments.

Keep in mind, your direction is substantial, and your sentiments are legitimate.

Find out about the various terms for directions. Figure out what they mean, and consider whether any of them impact you.

Consider doing additionally investigate by understanding discussions, joining LGBTQIA+ support gatherings, and finding out about these networks on the web. This could assist you with understanding the terms better.

Assuming you begin relating to a specific direction and later feel different about it, that is completely fine. It's OK to feel different and for your character to move.

How might I at any point be certain that my sexual orientation is gay?

That is an important question. Sadly, there's no ideal response.

Indeed, in some cases individuals truly do get their orientation "wrong." A lot of individuals thought they were one thing for half of their life, just to observe that wasn't accurate.

It's likewise conceivable to believe you're gay when you're really bi, or believe you're bi when you're truly gay, for instance.

It's absolutely alright to say, "Ohhh, I wasn't right about this, and presently I really feel more open to recognizing as X."

It's important for you to note that your direction might change over the long haul. Sexuality is fluid. Orientation is fluid.

Many individuals recognize as one orientation for as long as they can remember, while others carve out it changes over opportunity. What's more, that is Not a problem!

Your direction might change, yet that doesn't make it any less legitimate after some time, nor does it mean you're off-base or confounded.

Is there anything that 'determines' sexual orientation?

For what reason are certain individuals gay? For what reason are certain individuals straight? We don't have the foggiest idea.

Certain individuals feel they were conceived just exactly as they are, that their direction was generally only a piece of them.

Others feel their sexuality and orientation changes after some time. Recollect the thing we said about orientation being fluid?

Whether direction is brought about naturally, sustain, or a blend of the two isn't exactly significant. What is significant is that we acknowledge others as they are, and ourselves as we are.

How can this affect my sexual, and reproductive health?

Most sex instruction in schools centers exclusively around heterosexuals and cisgender (that is, not transsexual, orientation nonconforming, or nonbinary) individuals.

This lets most of us well enough alone.

It's critical to realize you can get Sexually Transmitted Infections (STIs) and, now and again, become pregnant paying little mind to what your sexual direction is.

STIs can move between individuals regardless their genital type.

They can move to and from a butt, penis, vagina, and mouth. STIs could actually spread through unwashed sex toys and hands.

Pregnancy isn't saved for straight individuals, by the same token. It can happen at whatever point between two individuals that have penis-in-vagina sex.

In this way, in the event that it's possible for you to become pregnant - or impregnate somebody - consider using contraception.

Who should I Involve Into My Sexual Orientation?

This is entirely up to you, and the people around you.

If you feel okay talking about it, to a friend, a stranger, a relative or family member, then you should. But remember that not telling anyone about your orientation doesn't make you a liar.

Any Implication For This?

Telling individuals can be daunting, yet keeping it hidden can be the same, as well. Everything relies upon your own circumstance, and your decision to involve people in it.

From one viewpoint, telling individuals could assist you with feeling better about your discovery. Many strange individuals feel alleviation and a feeling of opportunity once they come out. Being "out" can likewise assist you with observing a LGBTQIA+ people group that can uphold you.

Then again, coming out isn't always safe for you. Homophobia - and different types of fanaticism - are still very much alive and out there. Queer individuals are still victimized at work, in their networks, and, surprisingly, in their families.

In this way, while coming out can feel liberating, it's additionally alright to take things slow and move at your own speed.

How might I approach telling somebody?

Once in a while, it's ideal to begin by letting somebody know whom you know are open-minded and would not judge you, like a receptive relative or companion. In the event that you'd like, you could request that they be there with you when you tell others.

In the event that you're not happy discussing it face to face, you can tell them by means of message, telephone, email, or transcribed message. Anything that you like.

If you have any desire to converse with them face to face however are battling to propose the subject, maybe start by watching a LGBTQIA+ film or raising something about a known individual who is gay. This could assist you with information on how receptive someone is, and if you should go ahead, and discuss it with him or her.

You might find it helpful to begin with something like:

"After some events and much thoughts, and my own wild desires, I've realized that I'm gay. Yes, I'm attracted to men"

"Since we're close, I think it's important that you know that I'm bisexual. I'd love that you support me in that light."

"I've sorted out that I'm really pansexual, and that implies I'm drawn to individuals of any orientation."

You could end the discussion by requesting their help and guiding them to an asset guide, maybe on the web, assuming they need it.

There are numerous resources out there for individuals who need to help their queer loved ones.

Additionally let them in on regardless of whether you mind them sharing this news with other people.

How would it be advisable for me to respond on the off chance that it goes poorly?

In some cases individuals you tell don't respond the manner in which you need them to.

They might overlook what you said or dismiss it as a joke. Certain individuals could attempt to persuade you that you're straight, or say you're just not thinking straight.

In the event that this occurs, there are a couple of things you can do:

Encircle yourself with strong individuals. Whether it's LGBTQIA+ individuals you've met on the web or face to face, your companions, or open-minded relatives, attempt to invest energy with them and converse with them about the discovery.

Recollect that you're not the one off base. There is neither something wrong with you nor your orientation. The main wrong thing here is the bigotry.

They might need some time to process it, it's perfectly okay to give them space. By this, I imply that they might have understood their underlying response was off-base. Send them a message to tell them you're willing to talk when they've had an opportunity to deal with what you said.

It's difficult to manage friends and family who don't acknowledge your orientation, however it's soothing to know that there are many individuals out there who love and accept you.

Assuming you're experiencing the same thing - for instance, in the event that you were removed from your home or on the other hand assuming individuals you live with undermine you - attempt to observe a LGBTQIA+ cover in your space, or organize to remain with a steady companion for some time.

Where would I be able to track down help?

Consider participating face to face gatherings so you can meet individuals up close and personal. Join a LGBTQIA+ bunch at your everyday schedule, and search for meetups for LGBTQIA+ individuals in your space.

There's no simple, secure method for sorting out your direction. It very well may be a troublesome and genuinely intense interaction.

Eventually, the main individual who will mark your character is you. You're the main expert on your own personality. Furthermore, regardless mark you decide to utilize - in the event that you utilize any name whatsoever - it ought to be regarded.

Recollect that there are a lot of resources, associations, and people out there who will support and help you. You should simply make sense of them and reach.

CHAPTER FOUR

HOW TO FIGURE OUT IF YOUR FRIENDS, COLLEAGUE, OR FAMILY MEMBER IS GAY

Finding out whether or not somebody you're visiting or talking with (perhaps playing with, who the fuck even knows?) is additionally queer can be a goddam minefield. Certainly, certain individuals might have the guts to simply say it, yet not every person does alright?!

Here, 10 lesbian, queer and pan-sexual ladies make sense of how they know whether somebody's conceivably into them

The most effective method to know whether somebody is a lesbian, gay, sexually open or queer.

1. Pose An Inquiry About Their Past Relationships

"I'm sexually unbiased. I observe that I can see when ladies are into me through things like non-verbal communication, similar to how close they'll sit to me, how much they rub my arm. By flirtatious discussion, and clues/references to past lady friends, or female dates. I have no clue about how logical something like 'gaydar' is, yet I observed that I would frequently have this instinctive inclination that another lady was gay/sexually open simply through my initial discussions with them (and getting subliminal prompts in their non-verbal communication).

"Also, individuals have professed to have a similar sense about me too. So when I speculate it, I may very well pose an inquiry during the discussion that could assist with deciding it, such as getting some information about past connections they've had, or then again assuming they have any interesting tales about sex, and so forth"

Am I bisexual?

2. Simply Ask Them (Courteously)

"You can continuously politely ask them. It's a straightforward yet powerful method for being totally certain. I rather know whether somebody I may possibly be keen on is even open to the chance so I don't burn through my time."

3. Let Them Tell You

"She ordinarily tells me. I think this is a major difference between younger and more older sapphic ladies, yet as, I don't need to ponder nowadays. I out myself, they out themselves. At the point when you're more youthful and you feel like you need to ponder, I figure simply be forcefully out when you can and different ladies will too."

4. Hang Tight For Them To Make It Understood

"I'm horrendous at it. I don't feel like I deserve ladies, so I don't allow myself to accept they could be flirting with me. I generally legitimize it as them being agreeable. My ex went through weeks of stroking my hair, cuddling with me, and I 'coincidentally' brushed my hand over her boob. You know, similar to how friends do! In the event that I could travel once again into the past, I would be less stupid and simply ask her if she's into girls.

5. Get a Handle On Socials

"Online with dating applications - it's simple since they list their orientation. In real life - no sign except if they explicitly notice it. Simply need to feel it out like some other connection."

6. See How They Notice Their Exes

"Hard to discern whether she isn't obviously gay or queer. Normally the vast majority of my 'gaydar' goes at things like not commonly ladylike or essential. They either talk about their GF or female ex, or they don't discuss connections by any stretch of the imagination. Truly, every straight female I've conversed with recently either discussed their sweetheart, or their significant other, or a male ex."

7. They'll Give You a Grateful Look

"I can't characterize it, yet there's this look that gay ladies give out, an appreciation maybe. I've seen ladies on the train like this. Straight ladies NEVER take a gander at different young ladies like that level-headed. I would agree even something like their face structure, however that may be simply me."

You think you guy is a gay? You've probably been told that you baby boy acts 'funny and weird' in the presence of other men?

First clear your psyche and move past excessively moronic generalizations about gay individuals, and I'll give you my five findings:

8. Looking At Different Men

It is typical for each young lady to get irritated when her boyfriend, or even husband gazes at different ladies. Notwithstanding, presently you ought to be irritated or stressed when your man looks at different men. Nothing remains to be relaxed about this. What's more, there is a ton to stress over in the event that the hot folks you just saw has been deleted from your memory yet not from your sweetheart's.

9. No Sex In Your Connection

In the event that your man has been denying sex for at some point now, you can accept this as a sign. Indeed, even on unique days, in the event that he simply won't have intercourse to you, then he is avoiding any sort of actual contact. What's more, in the event that his reasons are 'tiredness' and 'headache' each time you take an effort at starting sex, it is about time you folks have 'the discussion.'

10. He Doesn't Recognize Hottest Young Ladies

For certain ladies it is a thing of pride to realize that her sweetheart isn't looking at different ladies. It brings them monstrous joy to realize that their person doesn't recognize ladies, not even the hottest ladies. Assuming that your man is cold and impassive in any event, when the most sizzling young ladies stroll by, this is a warning. Come on now, every man looks at hot ladies, and on the off chance that your man doesn't it has got nothing to do with reliability, it is something worth talking about to stress over his sexuality.

11. Anything You Truly Do Doesn't Turn Him On By Any Means

Each relationship has its special night time. There is the point at which you simply can't stop touching each another. Each touch prompts making out and afterward sex. Assuming your relationship never truly had that stage where your man would go all off the deep end on you, then this is one more sign that you really want to pay special attention to. In the event that he never gets turned on, regardless of what you do, there is plausible cause he is gay and you should rest assured about this assuming your person is touchy with men.

12. In The Event That He Shaves His Butt Opening

Men truly do shave their pubic regions. Indeed, even ladies do as such. However, who on earth shaves their butt opening? Assuming your person shaves his butt opening and keeps it clean the greater part of the times, you realize it is odd, particularly on the grounds that he doesn't allow you to contact him. This is a conspicuous sign that he may be gay and he is preparing himself for different men.

You may be heartbroken to discover this, however your partner may be having tougher time. Particularly in a general public like our own where gays and lesbians are not viewed as normal, you really want to extend your support. Converse with him about it and request that he come out. By doing this you will save yourself from being more heartbroken and you will likewise help him come out and acknowledge his own sexuality. Assuming you show him you are OK and open-minded, he will open up, else he will not and will simply lie about his sexual inclinations.

CHAPTER FIVE

5 things to consider before coming out as a gay person

Like most LGBTQ kids, you're somewhat anxious about coming out, isn't that so? All things considered, this is big news regardless of whether your folks have a suspicion about your character, it's something else to hear it from you. Lay the preparation now and you'll feel more quiet for moving toward into your life.

Consider these 6 things before telling your parents:

1. Pick The Perfect Set-Up Without Interruptions:

Make sure to have your parent's undivided attention before you start this discussion. Neither you nor your folks ought to be occupied with some other action (for example driving, cooking, staring at the TV, utilizing your telephone) when you come out. I likewise suggest that you don't share your news during other family occasions (like a wedding or dinner party). This is a private, cozy discussion that merits respect and calm. It will be difficult for your folks to completely assimilate everything you are saying to them on the off chance that they are not completely present.

2. Acknowledge That Your Folks' First Response May Not Be What You Had Trusted:

Recollect that you have had as long as you can remember to find some peace with your sexuality, yet your folks might not have really thought about it before you proposed the point with them. It is normal for guardians to have for you, and it might invest in some opportunity for them to feel alright with this new significant information you're sharing with them. Put yourself in their shoes, and imagine receiving that surprising news. Give them a chance to sit with this new information and do whatever it takes not to pass judgment on them (or feel decided by them) in the event that their first reaction isn't what you had envisioned.

3. Guarantee For Your Own Security And Prosperity:

On the off chance that, in view of their earlier comments or mentalities about the LGBTQ people group, you feel that your folks won't respond well, to such an extent that they will not endure your residing in their home as a LGBTQ young person, then I'd advice standing by to emerge until you are autonomous from your loved ones. This is particularly the situation on the off chance that your folks have a past filled with obnoxiously harmful or genuinely forceful inclinations. You should generally put your own security first. You can constantly "try things out" to check how your folks feel about others in the LGBTQ people group before you fire opening dependent upon them about this.

4. Be Extremely Clear About Who Your Folks Can Or Can't Tell:

I have heard many records of teens ending up being angry with their folks for "letting the cat out of the bag" about their sexuality or orientation. Whenever you emerge to family and dear companions, particularly assuming it is still almost immediately in your excursion, it is essential to illuminate whomever you trust in that they would be able or can't tell others. In certain circumstances, individuals let their folks know that they are gay and let them know that they are fine with their folks telling anybody they would like (truth be told, by and large, the youngsters incline toward this since it is one less possibly off-kilter discussion that they need to have). In different examples, be that as it may, individuals need to be in charge of precisely who is in on what they have viewed as confidential for quite a while. The primary message is that you can't anticipate that your folks should guess what you might be thinking so you ought to be exceptionally clear about with whom (if anybody) they are allowed to examine your sexuality or orientation, including your younger siblings, and family members from a parent's earlier marriage.

5. Empathize With Your Folks:

It could be difficult for your heteronormative folks to be best parent to a gay child, and this is best attributed to the fact that they've raised one or being with one before. Being a parent is the hardest occupation on the planet and your folks might not have peers they can go to for nurturing exhortation like they have before. Indeed, even guardians who have the best expectations will as often as possible "misunderstand entirely their lines" and offer something inadvertently hostile and terrible. At the point when that occurs, instead of answer with outrage, attempt and participate in a quiet discussion wherein you clear up for them what you want to hear from them and how they can make you feel accepted and loved in the family. We would say, many parents in all actuality do have unconditional love for their kids, however aren't generally ready to communicate that in a manner that is clear.

6. Give Your Folks Some Instructive Material:

Particularly in the event that your folks have no gay companions or other relatives, it would be really smart to furnish them with assets to assist them with bettering comprehend what you are going through and to help them during this possibly troublesome time. PFLAG or Guardians, Families and Companions of Lesbian, Gay, Sexually open and Transsexual Individuals, has assets you can download. Family Acceptance Project has accommodating exhortation you can show your folks too.

CHAPTER SIX

CONCLUSION

Loneliness doesn't segregate. Barely any individuals are adequately fortunate to endure existence without feeling secluded sooner or later. However, there are specific motivations behind why depression is predominant among the LGBTQ people group. Part of acknowledging you're gay, or bi, or trans, or non-double, or something besides cisgender and heterosexual is accepting you're unique and to an extent, separated from the majority. Numerous young LGBTQ individuals conceal their real selves from companions, family, and schoolmates before they come out, which is frequently an unquestionably detaching experience.

This feeling of detachment can be difficult to shake off, and it's additionally handily set off. Any place you live on the planet, but enormously the city, the LGBTQ people group is a dissimilar one highlighting bunch various clans. Observing your niche isn't simple all the time. Hitting the clubs can be an euphoric encounter, yet it doesn't be guaranteed to prompt long haul fulfillment. Madonna once sang, "I found myself in crowded rooms, feeling so alone," an opinion numerous LGBTQ individuals can connect with. Without a doubt, craftsman Richard Dodwell has recently published a compilation book, Not Here, committed to documenting queer dejection in the entirety of its structures.

You are beautiful, and your soul is beautiful. You are not perfect, just as all the other humans in the world. Regardless of what you've gone through, the bullies, the shamming, the hurtful words, losing friends and other horrible things that accompanied your sexual orientation, it won't still change the fact that you're trying, loved, appreciated and accepted.